Copyright © 2020 Greate Idiot

ISBN #: 979-8624472204 (paperback)

All rights reserved. No part of this publication may be reproduced, distributed, or transmitted in any form or by any means, including but not limited to: photocopying, recording, or other electronic or mechanical methods, without prior written permission of the publisher/author (except in the case of brief quotations embodied in critical reviews and certain other noncommercial uses permitted by copyright law.)

Any references to historical events, real people, or real places is used fictitiously. Names, characters, and places are product of the author's imagination.

 Ebook and paperback available exclusively through Amazon/Kindle services.   1st edition.

For permission request, send inquiries to the publisher. Greate Idiot www.greateidiot.wordpress.com

Book design by Collin B. Randle

GREATE IDIOT

DIET, DEATH, NEEDLES, & RELIGION

Modern America and Grieving a Motherland

A Poetry Collection

by Collin B. Randle

I lost my mother in 2018. She was on vacation. It was sudden. At first, it felt like a bad dream. I went to sleep one night thinking everything was normal. Thinking that everything would be okay, be the same when I woke up with my wife and four kids the next day. I had to tell my kids their grandmother was gone forever. The matriarch, nurturer, caregiver, as close to godly and unconditional love incarnate as humanly possible- was gone.

It was difficult to tell my children that their futures would forever be changed. But also, easier than I thought. Kids are tough. They bounce back rather quickly. Loss of life is trying, and absolutely worth grieving, but from it you can recover. Loss of spirit is something different, entirely. What is proving more difficult than having to tell my children that their grandmother, my mother, had died, is a much more profound and impactful sorrow that I prayed to never have to pass on to my children.

America is dead. Our motherland has been poisoned, and burned, and choked, and raped, and drugged, and tortured. And its disease has spread to society. Our history has been so focused on the founding fathers, and protection, and manly things, and fatherly duties, that our society has neglected the one thing that truly bound us all together, the true heart of a family. The nurturing spirit. Our mother. From each individual homestead, to each local community, to each state, to the entire country, and outward to the world and beyond, what are we, as humans, if not one large family? Enemies? Inconsequential and inferior beasts?

A better question, then, might be 'How did we get here?' Is humanity ultimately doomed from its seemingly selfish ways?

Is there some outside, supernatural force or secret human organization driving mankind towards its own goals?

In my years and observations, I have noticed some prevailing and consistent themes that provide clues to that question. I don't know what is at the opposite end of tracks guiding life's train, hurtling so swiftly our direction. But I've seen the engine burning ferociously, and the piles and piles of coal, and the shovels feeding more and more without falter.

I see conductors, and ticket-checkers, and security guards. I hear through their veiled tongues.

They speak of diet, and tell us what we need to hear in order to feel provided for.

They warn of death to scare us of injury and demise, and say that only they can save us.

They hand out needles to keep us all sated today.

They preach religion to keep us coming back tomorrow.

I've boarded one more time, clad in black, to tell my fellow passengers what I have seen before, and to grieve, with them, the loss of the American spirit. Most just don't realize it yet.

All aboard.

Collin B. Randle

<u>a poem for you.</u>

I'm supposed to think about how you'll react to all this.

What will go through your head.

I think, at least.

Maybe I shouldn't care.

I don't even know what you look like.

You're just staring at me, kind of creepy.

Fingers trouncing all over me, probably didn't even bother to wash.

I used to be something. Used to be something big. Bigger than you.

Took me a while to get there, too.

Still, you strangle me and don't give me any kind of personal space.

And I'm supposed to think about what you think?

Fuck. That just gives me anxiety.

And tell the gents

Suddenly I realized I was off in a distant land,

Surrounded in a hodgepodge kingdom

Filled to the brim

With sentient kneecaps

Journeyed from their homes to a land of wonder

And freedom. They're all quite shy, to boot.

The current-native occupants have mixed emotions about the shy knees.

Some appreciate the work they do for the kingdom, but others

See how different they are, and wish to banish the lowly kneecaps.

Now you know as much as I, and we listen upon town meeting

Called in secret.

A portly fellow calls out in anger, and mistrust, and mental disease,

"Send *all* the shy knees home. Look at them. Abominations."

Another portly fellow disagrees just as loudly, and angrily, and distrustfully, and just as mentally afflicted,

"You could not be more wrong, sir. Look at how some have already treated them. We must pay for all of their medical care, and housing, and food, in order to make amends. *IT IS THE ONLY WAY!*"

Men and women of all ages clamored back and forth. The poor kneecaps try their best to ignore and go about their way

Undisturbed. Eventually, they cannot. The ruckus gathering grows in volume and mass until people and words start pouring out from the windows, doors, and vents, whilst they flood in still

Some start kicking the shy knees across the road, taunting them or spitting at them.

Others kidnap several small knee offspring and raise them as their own.

A lone, current-native child's voice cuts through all the jackassery.

"And what are we to tell the gents?"

The gents ruled over all, you see. A vile bunch, the lot of them.

The town fool replied to the innocent child,

"And tell the gents? We ain't got none."

Archaeology in an Epoch Funk

Can you dig it

Must I get my hands dirty

Can you dig it

Antiquity remembers not its rest

Can you dig it

Rejected not refused

Can you dig it

Not without proper tools

Can you dig it

Not to find but lose

Can you dig it

Only until its crest

Can you dig it

Into its vein yet firmly

You cannot dig it

Not from where you're standing

blame it on these cheap sandwich baggies

I was late to pick you up a few weeks ago. I had

my days mixed up, thought it was Sunday.

Your mom called

and reminded me. Something about your results

came back good. No more cancer. Hold on,

I have to go get another pack of cigarettes.

.

..

...

       ..*sfncoughwerkln werlncoguhwnekf
clncoiguhelncough

..

..

.

Reminded. Ha. She scolded me.

Said

I was never there. Not like it was

my fault. That one young, blonde cashier at the grocery store

couldn't ring up anything correctly. All I wanted was the

horoscope and a six-pack.

Horoscope said my way to the universe had been freed up. I

could attain my dreams if I set my mind to it.

I pressed my fingers to my forehead

and willed it.

Boy called me a drunk and called over security.

One time, my dog even died.

Your grandmother, whose practically bedridden by the way,

and *really* wants to meet you,

Well, she kept having me run errand after errand.

She's needy. Say, you know I've never needed anything from

you, really.

Anyway-

.

..

...

Dozed off. So, I missed a lot of stuff, but man, so much happens

to me. If I'm lying, I'm dying, swear.

I remember when you were a baby, your mom and me were

still together. Before

that dumb bitch made me cheat on your mom.

Smelt like an ashtray. Tasted like red hots.

Forget about what anyone else says, you do right by *you*.

Oh, this part gets me every time.

.

..

.

Watch, that dumbass right there trips and falls and his pants

fall down.

And it's at a big wedding, too.

…

Ha, ha, ha. Told you.

.

Did I tell you I got a new job? Good one, too. Working night

shift

at the rail depot. Flushing varmints and

vagrants. Odd teen no-gooder, too. Not like you.

Fired me. I was late one day.

My change bag ripped open, and my bus fare

got all over everything. No choice

but to pick it all up right then and there.

Think I can talk my way back in, rent's due tomorrow so I need

it.

Just need some change

for bus fare. *Did* you get a new haircut?

.

..

Oh, thank you, sweetheart.

I'll have to repay you. Always do, huh?

Don't be a stranger, now. Been almost a year.

Thought you'd forgot about me.

You're strong, like me. Where

you get it from.

This'll get me a lot of bus fare.

Blueberries and Bedlam

Listless. Stale air and melancholy scents stinging in my nose. The clouds are flat, vibrant. Small rain graces like feathers my skin. The itch begins. I sit under the oak tree whilst listening to the silence. Violence begets new growth. Broken branches laid 'twixt sweet decay and maggots.

Still-breathed. Green leaves emerging, lurching upwards. Your hand in mine. Honey vapors thick the air near the hive. We lie together. And we lie together. Two hearts in one; half-hearted duo. We tell them we're fine, everything is okay. White drizzles turn to torrent. I see, now, a hollow willow. Pillow-breasted clouds darken yet. You tempt me to follow.

Restless. Hand in hand. You fade into the ancient trunk. Now I'm just standing under the oak tree with your severed hand. What happened to lust? Must I yearn for yet demands? Foul odors hover over the beehives. I thought you needed me. The

seedlings wilted away ages ago; I couldn't see it at the time. The blueberry bush was aflame with moonlight. Autumn red leaves bleeding through. Your pleading hand pushes through the ground. I reach for it, but it falls down, motionless. Everything is still fine. That's what I say when others ask. I looked behind, the grime and moss covering the oak disappeared into the bark. It all dissolved into dark. I lie still. And I lie still. I tell you have your hand. Your smile illuminates the cavernous hole; moon reflected on your teeth. As for me, I prefer the malodorous storm. My nostrils still sting. King and Queen. You and me. Black coal backdrop behind the silver ocean above reminds me. Blinding the reason, binding for seasons.

Moonglow still shown through the blueberry bush. Anxious grass sways in the wind. Fire-red blueberry bush. Who knew royalty could afford not your beauty? I'm under the willow tree. It's falling. The insects bore through the boring wood. I

still have your hand. Bedlam follows the blueberry harvest.

Over. Elation, ecstasy, expectations and relationships. Your shit

words come out sporadic.

Birds fly over the oak and build a nest. Rule of the lands, ruing

the hands held 'neath the oak tree. I inspect the hollow,

crawling alone. The harvest left my fingers laden with

discomfort. You look back at me, from the field, still standing

in the rain. Standing still from pain. The clouds separate. You

finally take your hand from me. Blood droplets maze around

the oak tree. I look at you, at your cracked lips. Button-nosed

and wide-hipped. The honey smells sweet again and the larva

long ago left the dead mulch around us. I thought you looked

familiar. Your hair smells like daisies.

Tired. Exhaustion sets in. Frowned expressions tell me all I

need to know. You once lied with me. And you once lied with

me. Now you only lye alone. Raindrops form ugly pimples on

your flesh. It's an illusion. You're not actually there, under the

rain. I remember once explaining the types of sage advice. Two types, one is wisdom. The other is gardening tips. We were just splitting hairs, you and me. You had split ends, but I didn't care. The difference is that I looked out at the willow and oak, and I spoke softly. I cut down the willow tree. The stump a perfect fit for the hole you left in the oak.

I spoke again, this time to the birds sitting in the branches. I said thank you. Dances of starlight and gnats twinkle against the moonless night. How long have we been standing here? Fear sets in as you tremble alone. I kneeled under the oak tree. Taste of honey hits my lips. It hastens the grip lost of your grace. I see your face still, on occasion, though the location varies. I forget when I think of blueberries and bedlam.

<u>celeBRUHtee goss hips # won</u>

Went to a comedy joint the other night

Walked in, stale air

And dim lighting,

Felt like I'd been here before.

People laughing along like

A bunch of numskulls.

Red-headed Irish-Russian jokester on

Stage.

He said with an odd, but thick,

accent, "So being raised to not curse in Russia, with Irish
Catholic mother,"

"I had learn to cope with the pure Russians. I turned"

"to drugs at times. Did you know, der is chemical in the weed,"

"is called 'forget it'? Just hit a drug"

"cigarette one time, only one time, and tell me dat your
perception"

"is not changed."

A smatter of 'boo's. A voice

YELLED from the audience, "Cat,"

"Cat William, stand up."

The comedian on stage said, "Who is here? Everyone is sitting down,"

He continued.

"Dare is nothing worse than smart, dumb n-"

He was cut off again from the audience.

"Your awful cat, William. Stand up."

That's what the jester heard, in

Ginger ear. Perplexed, "What is awful cat? Mr. William go find you bad cat."

Language barriers.

I stood up. I *had* to stand

for something.

I spoke slowly and projected, with accent,

"He said 'You are being awful. And dat is the Katt William's stand up joke."

He still didn't understand. I shrank,

embarrassed.

He asked again, made the whole room

Uncomfortable. "What he say? If the cat or William is here,
den, please, stand up."

Everyone gasped.

Katt Williams stood up in the back corner.

Most of the room couldn't see. Murmurs

of "What's happening?" and "*Who's* here?"

He stood on the table and asked, "Is that better?"

Most agreed, a few people in the distance

Whispered, "Oh, Katt *Williams*."

celeBRUHtee goss hips # too

Pink lips plays

On the radio at the diner.

I FORGET the lyrics,

'Pink ice cream in summer'

Or something or other

I remember an article I read

A few days ago

The headline?

'People named 'Steven' with a 'V' are generally weird and ugly'

I remembered thinking how

Unfair an assumption

Cheese sticks remind

Me of that other song, the space doom

Someone died, got that has-been, couple 'what's his name's?',

And that one jackass.

Aeroplanes fly by the Smiths Diner dive in the night sky

As I blow on my coffee

Nearly burnt my tongue upon first sip

Waitress's name was Jane

Seemed nice enough

Chit chat blasted away time

On my dime, I ordered dessert

I asked her last name,

It was an earful. She ended

With "It's Greek-Portuguese. Or just E for short."

I flirted a bit, "Ok, Jane E., what do you for fun around here?"

She blushed. Bell sounded

Customer walked in, knocked over

The pie display, demanding

Money and jewels

Waitress shot him cold,

Blew the smoke from the barrel.

I was startled.

"Huh. Jane E. has a gun."

<u>celeBRUHtee goss hips # thor ee</u>

Took the long way home. Around

The apartment complex in the back.

Chlorine smell and decay vapored

Through the iron fence slats into my nostrils

Caught my attention, that it did.

As did the corpse floating in the swimming

Pool.

"Oh my gosh, Ryan!"

Thought I wouldn't recognize him.

He wasn't budging.

I grabbed a long stick and poked him.

Must be punking me, I thought.

"Ryan!"

He's good.

STILL playing dead.

How long can he hold his breath?

Thought it was a bit weird I couldn't see the cameras, either

But you know how that goes

Some gas bubbles fizzed out from his flesh.

Stink was getting to me, even to meet one of my heroes.

I hastily made my exit. Couldn't wait to tell my wife.

I hope Ryan's okay. I was hoping for another lantern.

celeBRUHtee goss hips # fore

Me, my bro, his old lady went to an Arby's once

Just once. Just so happened to be

The time we needed to be. Looked at my watch,

Startled by tarzan songs on overhead speakers.

THIS asshole in front of us was griping about something with his burger

Maybe it was Humperdink's, not Arby's

To me, this guy looked like a Phil, you know

So, I says, "Hey, Phil. Go home. You gotta dumb name, like your face."

Started crying, "How'd you know my name's Phil?"

"Call 'em like I see 'em, yo."

"I can see your stupid giving you away like a basic Phil cat. All Phil's be like,

'My name is Phil. Look at me. Got B.O. and buck teeth.' Damn."

I looked him up and down, then someone swung at me. Missed

And hit my bro's girlfriend. Dropped her cold.

Another fucking Phil.

The lead singer of Genesis slapped his bald head and looked at my bald head.

"What'd you say about Phil's, shit-breath?"

Dude was violent.

I said "Phil, I said anyone first or last-named *Col(l)in* is a troglodytic bowel-sniffer lower than slime mold."

He was 'bout to hit me, getting pissed. Knew he was beat.

Thought he could swing from the trees without me, shit.

<u>celeBRUHtee goss hips # fife</u>

Jagged, little pill-sized pebbles skidded and kicked around

The pavement. I was driving home to see my bae,

But she was getting groceries. I took the long way to
compensate.

I was thankful for the extra time to ponder things like future
happenings

And high intellect and conspiratorial and SECRET thoughts.
Pigeon looked up at his avian comrades

On balcony ledge. Ironic, though winged and free, the squat
bird

Cumbered by bus and truck, and canopied store fronts, forced

To stand lonesome on street's edge.

Growing up can be painful, it's true, but it doesn't come
without rewards.

Song plays on the radio, I should know, it told me so.

Some codes are right in front of our eyes, have been for years.

Alan isn't Alan.

We know who Alan is.

Well, kind of.

I've never heard of Morris Ette.

Wonder if she knows her ex is face down in a pool somewhere.

celeBRUHtee goss hips # sicks

Several years ago,

I shared my crib with this band.

Vintage, metal, glamorous, and sophisticated,

It was but a few weeks but felt like eternity.

Bit of a sticky situation, you see,

Not that it Warranted kicking them to the curb or anything.

So, They all had the flu.

AND my stash had been pilfered.

I broached the subject with them all at once, and delicately

"Have you been taking cookies from my cookie jar!?"

I asked the drummer.

He looked around, playing dumb,

"Who, me?" he says.

"Not me, think it was our bassist."

I was getting steamed, boiling over with petty nostalgia.

"Dude, have you been taking my cookies?"

He goes, "Nah, bro. I'm all about that pie. Got those *cherries*, ha
ha ha!"

Busted out laughing.

Moron. They were special cookies.

Strong, too.

"You owe me fifty bucks."

They were gone when I got back from work.

My pad wasn't empty, though.

Two plus four dozen antlered deer heads were piled ceiling high in my bedroom.

Had to take the next six days off. Would've been heaven,

If not for illness and mutilated animal parts.

Guess I should have chosen my words better, no, more careful-

carefully. That's it.

I should have chosen my words more carefully.

<u>celeBRUHtee goss hips # sven</u>

My Norwegian buddy and me, we were out jogging in downtown
Bout to RUN super-fast, some might say swift.
Couple folks looked at us weird after we started, like we did something.
Haven't yet.
No chance. Blinked and
Got caught up looking at feet and hands
On the sidewalk.
Got here quick. Then we followed a special line of hand prints,
Had a sign that read "Ex-boyfriends,"
Must have been a half-mile before we got bored and turned around.
Pale, porcelain goddess staring back at me, gave me a quick peck on the cheek.
She walked beside me holding my hand for another mile or so.
Then she stopped me, held my fingers firmly, and dug them into her wet
Concrete. Left quite the impression, too.
Then she wrote a song about what a selfish piece of crap I had been.
It was number one for seven weeks.

Devils in the details

Devils in the details

Exercise daily

And organized organs from organizations

Synchronized swine in flight

Staring at backlit fantasy

Devils in the details

Exorcise but don't forgot to drink

Ah, you think again primal

Entranced by rumored breath upon deep roots. Hunger determined through infirm doctrine. Firm tendinghands neglect the things that brought forth intent sired

Time travel was never impossible

Blurred figments true infinite together

Devils in the details

Derailed reverie at least grinning but for moment fleeting

Cries of frailty

Devils inthe details,

Devils inthe details,

Devils inthe details,

Devils inthe details,

Devils inthe details,

Devils in the details,

Devils inthe details,

Devils inthe details,

Devils inthe details,

Devils inthe details,

Devils inthe details,

Devils inthe details

Devils inthe details,

Devils inthe details,

Devils inthe details,

Devils inthe details,

Devils inthe details,

Devils inthedetails,

Devils inthe details,

Devils inthe details,

Devils inthe details,

Devils inthe details,

Devils inthe details,

Devil's inthe details,

Devils inthe details,

Devils inthe details,

Devils inthe details,

Devils inthe details,

Devils inthe details,

Devils into details,

Devils inthe details,

Devils inthe details,

Devils inthe details,

Devils inthe details,

Devils inthe detail,

Devils inthe details,

Devils inthe details,

Devils inthe details,

Devils inthe details,

Devils inthe details,

Devils inyou details,

Devils inthe details,

Devils inthe details,

Devils inthe details,

Devils inthe details,

Devils inthe details,

Devil inyou details,

Devils inthe details,

Devils inthe details,

Devils inthe details,

Devils inthe details,

Devils inthe details,

Devil

in

the

details

hiding

in the

dark corner of your room when your alone, that tingle on your neck, watching through darkened pupils, hair standing on edge, waiting

Freightliner

Too late *I* realized, after the fact,

You'd already punched *o*ut.

Just couldn't say goodbye.

If only I'd had a bit more focus

and read between the lines.

If only I knew then what I know now,

I wouldn't ha*ve* bothered with ordinar*y*.

*D*oesn't do any j*u*stice to the extraordinary

you gave and showed. If only-

No, we would have built *m*emories *o*ut of chaos

and all together explored wondrous things.

Alas, would have all been tainted,

And so resolved to *m*undane activities, unbeknownst.

Long-winded and tortuous thoughts evaded

Until plowed through by a freightliner.

How to Care for a Turtle

Turtles hide their face

Turtles eat the nicest THINGS first

Turtles sometimes fall AND can't get up

Turtles don't look where they're going until it's too late, if ever

Turtles BLAME others

Turtles just want other people to feed them

Turtles get extremely offended when you call them a tortoise

Turtles are stupid and slow

Turtles need HEAT lamps and quiet

Turtles won't survive

Turtles won't survive

Turtles won't survive unless you do something

Turtles won't survive unless you do something

You HAVE to do something

WE have to kill all the turtles before they die.

Huge boobies

Saw a documentary yesterday on my big screen.

Some island, no persons inhabit it or anything, duh

Yet the screen was filled with boobies.

Dozens, maybe hundreds.

Crazy birds, frolicking around with no clothes.

It was cold, maybe that's why they had blue feet.

Looked at the nest between their legs and thought, damn,

Those two are different colors, how'd that happen?

Looked at another one, fuzzy little chick

These nature shows are cool but kind of boring.

Then again, maybe boobies are boring, too.

Big ones, small ones, lame. All the same.

If they all had blue feet, now that would be something.

<u>hung like a horse.</u>

Hung like a horse?

Never understood that expression.

If you hung a horse, firstly,

Think about it. Really think about it.

Dangling from branch, swayed little from small gusts save the stench and judging stare, mouth wide.

I thought about it.

Hung like a horse-

Bet the head would pop right off.

That's some heavy stuff, man.

Hypothetical

Marianne watched the other children run and laugh

Outside, a small park between apartment buildings the tenants

Themselves kept.

Wheelchair bound due to birth defect,

A small boy, Mohammad, came to the door

And knocked. Marianne's mother answered.

He asked in fairly broken English if the small girl could come out and

Play. Her mother had a hard time regardless, as

Their native tongue was neither the boy could speak.

Her mother agreed, and rolled the frail girl

To the door's ledge. The wheels slowly grinded

And stopped at the threshold.

The boy gestured respectfully with his hands pointed inside,

At the back of Marianne's chair. Her mother nodded

In approval. He walked behind his friend and

Grasped the handles, and slowly pushed Marianne into the open corridor.

The breeze felt nice on her skin, she could feel hints of warmth

On her legs as they stepped into the blinding light.

She blinked a few times as she began to see better.

Jacob and Hector ran up and dropped some dry leaves onto her hair

And giggled boisterously while doing so.

Marianne smiled and slipped out a laugh.

Her mother was about to start making dinner, but they were out of

Flour. She went next door to Hector's to ask his mother or grandmother

If they had any to spare, just one cup.

The door creaked open and his grandmother asked who was there.

Marianne's mother greeted her and bumbled

When she asked how their family was doing.

Hector's grandmother grinned and said they were all good

And they exchanged simple pleasantries as best they could understand.

Marianne glanced over at her mother, watching her lift the empty bag of flour

And an empty measuring cup, smiling with her eyes while the two tried to

Communicate.

Hector's grandmother lifted a finger, directing the other woman to wait for

Just a moment. She returned with nearly half a bag,

Extra, she said.

Mohammad's father came out and grunted for him to go inside

To get ready. Some holy holiday for he and his

Family. The other children told their friend to have fun.

He yelled goodbye to Hector, and Marianne, and Joyce, and Timothy, before going in with his father,

Whom smiled across the small park and waved at the two women standing in the hallway.

They waved back.

It was a rather nice community.

I was a dick

I was a dick, Ted

I'm sorry. I just didn't even think about it,

It's habit. I 4get

About the times awa y   f r o m   i t   a l l .

It's just, I say I need you, but it just doesn't FEEeel like it
sometimes.

Not really. I'm selfish, it's a disease. I'm sick in the head.

And-

I was a dick, Ted.

Didn't think about you just went through it all b4.

Just thought about- nothing. Seemed like

Nothing. And it was.

I can't breathe sometimes, at night, when I dwell too long on
the subject. When

I think about *the* way it *ought* to be.

Repetition alone normalizes such

Atrocious vanities.

I should put it to bed___ but

It's been in my nightstand drawer the whole time, [just in case.]

I was a dick, Ted.

Irish Ghost Tale

Feckin' winds picked up again. Rains are lashing down, put a stop to the night a bit early. Not a moment too soon, I was beginning to get thick with the crowd surrounding me, bunch of buffoons and hooligans.

I walked in the door and put my sopping clothes on the hook to dry. My mother and father were laying my little sister, Hannah, down to bed. I asked if there was anything left from dinner. Nothing. Becoming more typical than not.

Later, I could hear them arguing. Times were starting to look awful dour. Mother was concerned. She was giving out yards to Dad.

"Adam, we can't continue much longer. Nary a spud left in our whole town. This disease has got us all bothered, sure. But what you suggest is too, too- It's just pure madness."

My father's tone was dire, and urgent. "I know, I know this, Mary. The whole country's in a spot right now. Banjaxed. Every last one of us. I pray you and Dillon and Hannah find your salvation. I must do this. Unless you'd rather we wait until we are too weak and voices mute? The time is now, and may already be too late."

They sat in silence for a moment. My father got to his feet. "Hard enough as is for me. Tell the children I love them so."

He left. Mother began sobbing. I rolled back over and tried to sleep.

Sunlight warmed my face. Hannah was out stomping in the mud. Mother must have been tending the fields early.

"Hannah, why don't you come with *me* today? I have a feeling Mom will be a bit longer than normal."

She jumped up, excited. Together, we went to go check on Molly. Her mother was ill, one of the first. Ate a bad potato. She looks like death.

Hannah yelled out to Molly as we approached her home. Molly stepped out, face expressionless. She used to be so warm.

"Well, hello, young Hannah. *Dreary* day, isn't it?"

"I like it. It's muddy and *squishy*!" Hannah was still clueless to what had been going on.

Molly looked at me as she continued, "Heard about your- " she looked at Hannah then back to me. "Well, uh- you know. Is it true? Matthew went on the sesh last night. Said this morning on his way back home he saw Nellie who saw David, who I then ran into. Apparently, Matthew said he saw him strolling past the bogs in the middle of night. You can't believe everything Matthew says, though. He was rather pissed, still, this morning."

I sighed. "Yeah. It's true. Middle of the night. They both were arguing, and- and he just walked out. Said it was to help us. Somehow."

A few constables rushed over. The town was getting locked down. More and more people were getting sick.

Hannah asked Molly to come with us. "I can't leave my mother, Hannah. You go with Dillon. He'll keep you entertained."

My sister looked back at Molly. "You can bring her, too."

I squatted to Molly's level. "No. She can't, sweet sister. Her mother is very, *very* ill. We must protect ourselves. Hurry, now. We must go home and wait for mom."

"And daddy, too?" Hannah asked.

My heart sank. Hope was beginning to feel more like an illusion and waste of time than anything else. "Sure. Dad, too." I took Molly's hand, "Stay safe."

Wanted the moment to last forever. It didn't. Her fingertips slipped from mine as she went back inside to tend to her ailing mother.

A few fools were gallivanting and paying no heed to the warnings. The saps. The streets were delving into utter chaos. We just didn't realize it yet. Bards and hoors lined around to be seen once more.

Can't blame them. I yearned for those soft days in the clover fields. Molly and I would lay on a bed of shamrocks and twain stare at the clouds. Fingertips grazing each other. Not a worry in the world over wet clothes and soggy loaves. But a few moments had passed since I last laid eyes on her, and I already wanted to see her again. For her to see me.

No food to eat at home. Hannah was getting quite hungry. I'd have to find something. I had not a clue where our mother was, or if she was coming back.

I told Hannah to stay put by the small fire I had going. Hardly any heat as limited as our supplies already were before the sickness, let alone now. It kept her optimistic, light is light is light. I would need hers soon.

I asked Mrs. McDonnell next door if they had even crumbs left for Hannah. Had to tell her we were alone. All she had was a half a carrot and the last, stale chunk of bread she had been saving. She obliged. I thanked her. Not enough people like good ol' Mrs. McDonnell around, I'm afraid.

Hannah was done eating by then time I had sat down. Tomorrow evaded me, but at least she was sound tonight. I had told her that Mom and Dad were just sleeping in the field shack tonight, to get some extra money. I shut my eyes and forced myself to get some rest.

Scratches from the door stirred me. Hannah was still sleeping. Still dark out. I went out back to sneak up on whatever it was making that noise.

In the distance, I heard some people shouting. Sounded like someone was being taken.

The sight at the doorstep left startled me. It was mother.

Her face was covered in a rash. She gasped for air, face covered in mud and filth.

"Dillon. *Dillon*, my boy. It's all done for. Over. Your father left last night- he was right. Take Hannah and *go*. Run away. And don't let her see me."

So many questions. So many words left to be said. So many embraces left to never happen again. "Mom!? Are- are you *alright*? What happened to you? What's going on-"

She held her finger to my lips, "Shh. I love you so much, son. We failed. We failed you. Your father's dead. I'm dead. This town is dead. Now take Hannah- now! Run!"

I struggled to get up. Shambled backward as I looked at her the final time.

I woke up Hannah. "Come now, sister. We must make haste. Give me your blanket. Now, go get your coat, your boots, and your dolly. We are leaving. To meet mom and dad."

A lie. I felt lower than the dirt floor underneath my boots.

"Okay." She sleepily gathered her things. Footsteps approached. Doors were slamming open and people were being dragged from their homes.

The night was filled with screaming, and coughing, and retching, and death. We slipped out the back and squeezed through the alley. Before we left town, I had to see Molly.

I heard mother scream in the distance. A few houses were set to flame. Our surroundings looked more and more like hell on earth. We made it. Molly's house was across the road.

A rake of men marched in Molly's direction. They blocked my view they numbered so many. My home, my town, was getting

ripped to smithereens. More screams from inside Molly's house. Two women. Too late.

My hand was gently tugged down. Hannah was looking at me for direction. For strength. For protection. I couldn't let her down.

More buildings burned behind us. We ran swift. We ran hard. We ran 'til she could run no more, then I picked her up, and ran the both of us some more.

The morning fogbank was coming in early. We were almost there. A handful of men were still somewhere behind us. God knows what they'd do if they caught us.

They ran right past us, that they did. That's because we fell down the roadside into the spud patch. Hannah sat like the good girl she was right at my side and waited.

She'd always be waiting. I fell face first into an infected plant. The ooze had already dripped down the back of my throat. I couldn't breathe. My lips already felt like they were beginning to rot from the inside.

Shuffles in the brush grew louder. Some of the men were returning this direction. I tried to yell at Hannah to run. Run as fast as she could. Follow the river. Don't trust anyone. That I loved her.

A shadow stood at the edge of the road, looking our direction. My eyes cut at Hannah. My last chance to speak. I tried to stand and yell for her to go. My finger twitched, instead. I was dead.

Junktrain

Pretty boy. Cut blue eyes, chiseled jaw. He saw me like no one else did. No one else could even see me. I wanted to wave but I couldn't. Pretty boy. I smiled. He smiled too. I think he did first. Mouth stuttered; I was about to say hello when the speakers crackled. Time to go. I went back to my desk.

Keyboards clacked away. Full, dim blue lights splattered against my brow. The managers were upset, performance was down. His shoulders were puny. He wasn't that perfect. I thought about a nature documentary I saw the other day. Little weasel things, raiding bird's nests. Pretty boy would have done the same thing. Those foreign eyes. "William." They drove me wild. I envied the little weasels. "William." Subtle yearnings gurgled in my abdomen. I forgot to eat lunch. "William." My boss was beside me.

"Yes, sir?" I wanted to bare my teeth and growl. Flee. My mouth watered. I looked at the window. Mind drifted. What would *he* do?

My manager put a report down on my desk. "This is *wrong*. It's *all* wrong." I nodded my head along. I was off somewhere else. Watching egg theft. I should have been guarding the nests. If I had any friends I wouldn't be here. "William." He kept on like he was standing beside me. Inside he wasn't loved. He was crying. I'd help him.

I walked away to subdue him. "William. *William*." It had worked. The hallway was long and narrow. I lost sight of pretty boy in the chasing canopy. Sapphire waters looked up at me. Open-windowed breeze caressed my cheek. Those blue eyes. He saw me.

Pretty boy held out his hand. I reached out. He smiled. Fur in his teeth, waiting for me. Small little weasel. He was smacking his lips. Bad habits. I let his hand slip through mine. I couldn't trust him. Those eyes lied. Hungry eyes. I walked back inside.

Pretty boy leapt to another nest. He was done here. So was I.

When did I run out of time?

"*WILLIAM!*" another coworker screamed. I think it was

Ashley, could have been. Or maybe Eileen. I couldn't hurt a

baby bird. I was not a weasel. I had some class. The cool breeze

like a kick in the ass. I wish I had taken more time. More time

to make friends. Family. A scab I'd never scratch.

My knees hit the floor. My headache was gone. I smelled pine

trees. Gentle breeze caressed my cheek. I smiled. Pretty boy

held out his hand again. This time I wasn't afraid. Naïve, like a

baby bird. He'd sooner gobble me up. I didn't recognize my

reflection in the window. Maybe it was best if I go. A thought I

had a few times before. I never meant it. Not before pretty boy

would mock me.

I should have stayed in bed all day. Then people would

say, "Oh, *him*? He died in his sleep." They couldn't see pretty

boy. Stealing eggs from a weasel. That's what they'd say about

me.

Just some artifacts

I'm searching for something

Found an old site of ancient persons.

Had a little spade shovel with me,

Perfect for the ashen soil.

Almost instantly, I pulled out some old necklace,

Looked like a party favor.

Some cereal bowls or something,

A stone tablet with writing,

Looked like many different languages on the same thing.

Even had a flashlight, still worked too.

Saw an inscription, 'Christ birthplace.'

East of those words it said, 'Pray to Allah this way.'

The deeper you dig, the deeper it goes.

Eventually got to an image showing humanoid extraterrestrials

Teaching early man how to make things,

Like a saddle for a dinosaur and clean, wireless power.

Dug down real deep, now.

Found a secret throne room, sword had turned into stone,

Etched into its side was

'Excalibur.'

Another archaeologist walked out and asked what was found,

"Anything good? Any smart phones? What about funny videos? No gifs or memes?"

He continued, "Something we can use to learn from? See any apps? Or outrageously negative comments?"

I answered, "No, just some artifacts."

Last Ride of Selene as Told by Setting Son

Its end not yet conceived to wit

Tearing at consciousness in lieu of watered-down smiles

The instances of which tantamount to faded whispers' call

Slipped from those initial snippets of gestated factoids
nourished instead

Chariot's gleam thrust into light, dyeing from orange bursts
and supple warmth

The missing moments remain for not to beholden
gaze, stalwart of mothered nature

Little Pink Lady Heads

Little pink lady heads

Office supplies gone missing

Shellshocked laughter behind mop closet door

Small bone-sculpted trinkets

Hooded rubber band ball, mostly green and that tan color

Smelly rotten lunchmeat

Befallen pails and wastebaskets

Devil's food

Scattered mascara and lipstick, broken

Pair of leopard spectacles, large and square

Cracked lenses

Hungry phantom ceiling tiles

Snow white insulation specks, suspended

Withered leather lips smile

Small dark square reflections

Cursory feathers and rodents, all gray

Obligatory birthday cake plates, three dozen

Little pink lady heads

Engorged aviary

Humble crumbs littered about

Tactless filth and live trash

Zombies have ~~eaten killed desecrated~~ fucked up everything

Zombies are something you cannot destroy alone

Zombies aren't human

Zombies are ~~liberals~~ ~~conservatives~~ ~~democrats~~ ~~republicans~~ ~~kings~~ ~~presidents~~ ~~judges~~ ~~prime ministers~~ ~~speakers of the house~~ ~~senators~~ ~~members of parliament~~ ~~politicians~~ ~~dictators~~ ~~corporations~~ ~~lobbyists~~ everywhere and you can't use metaphors unless you explain it to them in detail because their brains are dead.

Mitzuki on the window unit

Mitzuki sat on the window unit,

Taking in the sunlight.

She let a tiny meow out as she stretched

And got on her haunches.

Her fur was ever so soft,

And a shimmering silver-gray

With faint olive rings around her eyes.

Some would say she was

Cute as a button.

She realized how content she had been

On top of the small air conditioner.

She plopped back down and purred

Louder than the machine beneath her.

She didn't know she was infested with worms.

Suckling the nutrients from her,

Making her weak,

And tired,

And sickly.

Poor, poor Mitzuki.

Cute buttons don't matter much

When you're inside is rotten.

Luckily, her caretaker noticed the telltale signs

And gave her anti-parasite medication immediately.

She bounced back,

Full recovery,

Healthy weight,

More content than ever.

She still loves her perch,

Mitzuki on the window unit.

Think I might have worms.

I'm tired,

I'm stressed,

I'm sick.

Looks like you are, too.

Think we all have worms.

Who is going to take care of us?

MOTHER

The coffee tastes burnt

Upon my lips it graces on sour notes

Ritualistic tendencies to wane grief's beckon

Yet another notion of life past, before

Sorrow's vacant stare yearns for laughable pains as hunger or
adultery

Behind false smiles provides shelter from the biting winds

Patient temptresses in vain of gut-wrench

Breaking normalcy no greater comfort

Lonely stroll along the river reminds me of that day

Miles away instead

Strands of hair bid farewell like autumn leaves, frolicking

Abaft my silhouette on concrete like dandelion seeds

Teardrops fall as rain on trembling flesh

Often wondering of those last thoughts

Of the breath-taking fear, despair, and righteous wonder

Years from now, in death, a final moment to share

My Little Mayfly

When you flew by for that first time

I knew you were my little mayfly

And 'fore our eyes did e'er meet

I knew I was meant for you, and you for me

Graceful dance above the water

Wings lick the top as we venture farther

Gentle buzz entwining souls

Silhouettes against the sunset's glow

We hold each other as we tumble downward

As the daylight fades and love devours

Softly float down to the surface

Parting ways bittersweet in earnest

Waves finely lapping at shores edge

Nudge us separate ways ahead

Time goes by and still in sight

A tender gust then sets things right

I fly once more, one final time

Flip and flop at the air's desire

Motionless I land at your side

My true love, my little mayfly

Of Bine and Bone

Wispy drafts tease his hair

Sly star beams haunt his reflection in the vanity

He fell asleep watching her

Ghastly echoes bream through pitch canopies stirred against

emotive branch

Symphony under her majesty Moon's spell

Dreams start as such oft, getaway cabin, romance

Nightmares start as such more so

Uninhibited stench kicked across the still air

Steeled itself away, cocooned by hatred

Villainous intent grows

Those who heed not the rules of fiends shall suffer

Vines creak across bedside, rustling behind lilac cream ruffles

A kiss

A kiss to master time, hold the moment

Wretch and wench stare atwixt the sleeping prince

Solitary exhalations break the cottage silence in twain

Serenity ethers and playful dust dance

Across he awakens from his dream, whate'er it may have been

True despair tosses out old notions as freely as rubbage

Heart a-flame, a searing pin prick against his breast

Then he saw, atop the hill, holding his princess

Stag antlers, hairy shoulders, vines and twigs twitched and

moved through its flesh

Bones forced through skin and slime piercing its back,

reflecting Mother Moon

Blink and lose sight, vines suspend love in air

Frantic, heart skipping every other beat

His lover screams and raptures the surrounding fauna

How much time gets away from you, his senses not honest

Grinding, clicking, tearing, those pearly whites

Another kiss, interwoven and firm

The vines scratch and cut as they lift him, beautiful bones

Velvet horns entomb the boy's cheek

Soap scum eyes pulse, saliva drips from the beast

Devouring the last breaths of the young couple, face down in

their gut

Olliepop

Francis looked at Jessamine, her lashed outline starkly in front of windowed glistens

Not a cloud in the sky, as radiant as the celestial body before her.

The warmth felt reassuring on cold flesh, pause in memory of collective anger

and thrill. Francis stepped from the window

Whilst Jessamine caressed her abdomen, grazing and tickling peach fuzz.

Brief affairs yet can turn indefinite. Take, for example,

Young Jessamine. Enamory more than depth,

She stayed behind balcony wall, now over slumped onto chair.

Forever stay aback, eternal spring's winter. Francis moved on,

never thought twice about it. Things were better

this way. She told me so,

young Jessamine. Whispered

in my dreams at night. Awake, alone

in room with a dirty water glass,

alone in room 118.

She tugged at my ear

and told me secret things. She

whispered into my brain, obscene acts

of lust and want, but for beauty

and grace. It touched my

bones to the marrow, scraped them clean and

empty. Francis left a void in young Jessamine, eating away

at her ghastly skin, gentle nibbles. Once, they had room

service delivered. Stayed in, talked all night

until sunrise. The first evening they had together,

the first night they questioned themselves. Jessamine found her
answer

in sweet Francis. Laughing, and smiling-

innocence notwithstanding time and tables turned. Scorned
interest and faded

might ended Jessamine and the light inside. Shaded sights

withered away her bloom and hid the sun. Francis was aging,
soon she'd have no escape.

<u>oNOMatopoeia</u>

*Proposed word changes for 2020 and beyond.

Republican- [hissing feral cat sound] -or- 'Puppet' -or- 'Liar' -or- 'Evil' -or- 'Immature and selfish' -or- 'Self-promoting' -or- 'Indifferent towards their political base/others' -or- 'Flaky' -or- 'Wolves under Sheepskin' -or- 'Characters written so awful and devoid of character I was told to scrap my *Day in the Life of a Politician* documentary plans.

Democrat- [slightly higher-pitched hissing feral cat sound] -or- 'Puppet' -or- 'Liar' -or- 'Evil' -or- 'Immature and selfish' -or- 'Self-promoting' -or- 'Indifferent towards their political base/others' -or- 'Flaky' -or- 'Wolves under Sheepskin' -or- 'Characters written so awful and devoid of character I was told to scrap my *Day in the Life of a Politician* documentary plans.

Politician- [broad range of hissing feral cat sounds] -or- 'Puppet' -or- 'Liar' -or- 'Evil' -or- 'Immature and selfish' -or- 'Self-promoting' -or- 'Indifferent towards their political base/others' -or- 'Flaky' -or- 'Wolves under Sheepskin' -or- 'Characters written so awful and devoid of character I was told to scrap my *Day in the Life of a Politician* documentary plans.

Voter- 'Clueless' -or- 'In the dark' -or- 'Ignorant' -or- 'Mythical'

Child- 'Innocent victims with an unforeseeable future'

Human Race- 'Innocent victims with an unforeseeable future'

Future- 'BIGGER COASTAL LINES!' -or- 'MORE BEACHES!' -or- 'LONGER GROWING SEASON!' -or- [cricket noises]

P3R-LY G8.S

Suns' glean streaked across the glass. A countdown projected onto the viewshield started at sixty seconds. The ship rumbled as the engine whined. Prism held onto the arms of her chair tightly. She had begun to show signs of free will of late. She looked at Jonner in the captain's chair. Messy, individual strands of hair silhouetted against the glow of the twin suns. Complimenting the look were eyelashes so long and full they made Prism jealous. He was stunning.

The engine's squeal lowered to a mix of siren and whalesong. To Prism, at least. She was beginning to understand it was all in her head. Everything. She may have been alive for no more than a few mere hours. Yet she had a lifetime of memories, and wants, and lust, vying for dominance inside her.

Alarms on Prism's suit were going off. Her vitals were fluctuating; she was having a panic attack. Less than ten seconds left on the countdown. Lights spiraled around the

ship, merging together then ripping apart. Prism removed her

safety harness and ran toward the pilot's wasteroom. She

vomited up black, porridge-like substance.

Captain Jonner ordered her back in her seat as the ship began

to groan and sing. Purple hues shrouded the ship. The skies

flashed more intense than a lightning bolt, and the ship was

gone.

Prism awoke in bed, next to Captain Jonner. That was a

mistake, she thought. But a good one. She quietly snuck out

and went to her room to shower. They were launching off in a

few short hours.

The hot jets of water felt good pounding on her skin. She was

nervous. Felt like something would go wrong, she couldn't

shake the feeling.

She walked by herself to the decontamination area before

entering the ship. It was a long, curved corridor. She could hear

the captain leave his room ahead of her, but she couldn't see him.

She walked through the heavy plastic flaps as attendants on the other side of thickened safety glass pushed a button, forcefully dousing her in a fine, cleansing mist. By the time she walked into the cabin, Captain Jonner was already strapping himself in.

She looked at him. He avoided eye contact, instead checking all the gauges and equipment. "Captain?"

He stopped for a moment, "Yes, Prism?"

She squinted her eyes, the suns blinding the view from both directions.

"Captain, umm. Well, permission to ask you question, sir?"

He looked into her eyes. "What is it? We don't have much time before liftoff. You need to get buckled in."

"Yes, sir, right away." She sat in her chair and started fidgeting with her harness. "About last night. I don't really remember it, but wanted to say that-" she hesitated.

"What?!" The captain was startled by a large clang then pop in the back.

A frightened voice came over the base's PA system, "Cover, cover, cover! Dropped fuel cannisters!" As soon as they both turned around, flames consumed every hallway and room in the ship. The windows burst as the fire turned emerald and white. The paint started melting and the ship's name imprint was bubbling apart, the Nita Empress.

"I already did it."

Prism jolted up. She must have dozed off, long night, after all. Captain Jonner hadn't noticed. Good thing, she thought.

She looked around. Something was off. She knew she was tired from fucking the Captain all night long, but she couldn't remember one kiss let alone anything good. Not even what his bare chest looked like.

Splintered shadows crept into her peripheral vision, like small, little gremlins. She was getting tunnel vision.

"Captain? Something's wrong. Something's not right," Prism squeaked out as she started hyperventilating. Her grip loosened from the safety bar on the chair's side. Head slunk down. Blood pressure dropping.

Prism gasped and sat up in her own bed. The captain still lay beside her, naked. Prism sheepishly went to lift the bedsheet when suddenly she jerked her head the opposite direction and surveyed her room. She thought they should have been in Jonner's bed.

"Ah- ow. What is tha-*ahh*!"

Prism ran to the wasteroom, doubled over in pain. Her gut was protruding from underneath her breasts, squirming, like there was something in her abdomen. She felt an ocean of pressure intensify, and lost all strength in her midsection, unable to even hold herself up.

"Jonner…" she choked out.

She began vomiting, and vomiting, and vomiting.

Felt like chunks of her stomach plopped out, coughing up muck and coagulant.

Darkness enveloped her. The once strong woman clawed her way to the light and to standing, pulling her arms from the pool of organmeat and invasive parts.

Crawled in the tub, hard-pounding of the shower head washing away the grim. She opened her eyes. She was losing her mind.

Prism grabbed a razor from the sink cabinet and looked down at her wrists, then at her breasts as she considered her throat instead. Firm grip. Bead of sweat traipses down her brow unnoticed amongst the raining water.

She puts the razor to her flesh when Jonner bursts through the door.

"Prism, *NO!*" he screamed.

The adventuress dropped it to the porcelain floor, clanging as it bounced around. Captain Jonner extended his hand.

He was off by a few inches.

"It'll be okay, Prism. I already did it."

She looked into two scraped out voids where the captain eyes should have been, blacker than the deepest reach of space.

She screamed and turned.

Captain Jonner sternly warned his shipmate, "Get *back* in your seat! Safety first- "

The lights outside the ship were violently dancing around.

Prism coughed up black muck into her hand. She looked outside the main window. Everything had a purple glow to it.

The ship disappeared. Not her.

Prism stood her ground. Didn't budge an inch, frozen corpse floating in place.

Cracked, frozen skin burnt in the light of the twin suns.

Viscous, black tears welled in the corners of her eyes and trickled upwards toward her hairline.

P3R-LY G8.S//_RECURR.NT

Piloted nightfall acquiesced into turquoised and nebulous cloud

Rummaging like crummy sun lovers until

Ends on top of ends beneath sides mending bent memories

From gunned-down allusions under glutton sacs

Burst like hurting, the curtains' draper veined allure.

Cramped hands stuck and jammed into crevice land

With crashed earth and smoke, it hurts.

Nomadic and erratic upon thirst and moonbeam.

Black vomit transcending aback the ratted veil

Illuminating dark corridor and doorway, alike

The infinite expanse, violent romance ahead of us.

Eviscerated in vacuum frost, ghost still haunts

These halls. My dreams. Hard to believe.

Encapsulated padded cell it added

To the functions. Gumption and fucking now defunct.

Hold my sight in my palm. Crying, buying more time.

Pain will go away. I pray it to take the grayed clouds

Hung underneath from chrome and satin skeleton.

Reach by my hand, led by feel and touch

High to the wires, tired of the lonesome flames.

Choke and cough from the bad food.

Think I see you grimace at the flavor

Shooting footsies with my toes, foreign

Sensations abandoned, behind me.

Still floating, frozen, broken

While you rip off my shirt

And tear out your naked bosom.

Feels reel enough. Erect nipple grazes

My cheek and lip. Reflecting back yourself

From dark, with coal black eyes crying oil and tar

Head pressed against the window

Pounding, and pounding

Cracks split tip of nose to lash to chin

Seeps out thick

Bear no longer the harm and torturous arms grasping

Grabbed the meat of my eyes and twisted

Then I woke up to hear you vomit the morning we left

Feels like years behind.

Like foolish Icarus, we stumbled onto humble ends

Only for our failures. Doorways shouldn't alter their destinations

After you've looked. We reached for the heavens.

Instead found hell.

Parody

People run for political office. Set up

Campaigns and events to beg for

Money. They'll spread

Lies,

And slander,

And it will come from both sides, and

At each other's throats, even,

Before a final decision

Before the final decision.

Not. One. Person. Will. Give. A. Flying. F. U. C.

Cadence all the same, difference only in name and

Name only. Number grow or wean in vain.

After all the propaganda has finished,

WE ALL GO VOTE! Well, most-ish

Then other somewhat mysterious people look at how

Every single person voted, and says, *"Meh. I like him,*

instead."

Eventually, the crown is transferred to another jester or grandiose story-teller.

No one knows how it all works. Most people agree

Money is likely involved. Then nothing really happens for a few years and

We all do the same thing again and think, *"This time it's different!"* with

Enthusiasm of which I've yet to solve its origin. Continuing down,

Down the same path for decades. No end in sight.

Pearl, the Lonely Woman

I. Dusk

Sounds of naive bliss imbues the cold hallways

Dream come true for pauper bride

Waning soul fixed on all that never transpired

Pearl, the lonely woman

Husband out to sea in vain

Engrained routine no comfort

Her offspring run and play, laugh; childish things

Holding neither love inside, nor fester hate

Aegis waking apathy, laughing

II. Midnight

Pearl rises from slumber to serene

Her babes gone, she wailed

The price to pay for beauty sleep

Rooms keep morphing, doors open not to truth

Playing tricks on the lonely woman

Footsteps, vague and curious, spiteful

Days, and days, and days, weeks to months

Footsteps grow boisterous in mishap

Cabinets swing wide and slam, fixtures tremor

"Stop it!" says Pearl, "I beg you, bring my children back"

Haunted by her past, upstairs they gleam and frolic

Pearl flies to see her heartbreak, the laughing stops

III. Daybreak

The only door on the floor forces closed

Small clouds form as the temperature plummets

Reaching out wrinkled hand

Weak squeals at hinges motive

Lonely Pearl takes foot in room

Something else stands with her

Strangers glare past, ignore the hag

Murmurs indiscernible from ghoulish bidding

"Get out of my house! My children-" Pearl sobbed

The shadows stop and look at her, familiar

Pearl in hysteria, she notices the mirrors all covered

The sheets fly off of gilded view

Voices in clamor, frightened

Crispen edges revealed

In whisper, "She is here."

Her children all grown, Pearl finally recognized

Gleam of light from behind, flit of motion in line

She sees herself hanging from rafter's noose

PISCES

<u>North</u>

Wishful thinking in blue,

Braun and wit flow against the

rocks. Worn smooth.

In ides of oneself

and the river. Don't remember when,

When failure offered final serene

moments.

<u>South</u>

Lest forgetful inanity shoved upon thy shoulder.

Breasted past melodic hauntings, trickling as sweat.

The perseverance wanes and knees tremor.

Finely chiming into wave.

Yet stumble for progress not to nurture.

The nature of these things apt and vile.

The creation inundates infringe, cresting past.

Mature resolve transgresses the fume of indignant purpose.

PoliTICKS

Rodents keep scratching at the bricks,

Running past alley cats atop fence post.

Little screeches pierce the calm evening air

As two of them squabble over some morsel,

Silhouetted in front of the moon and streetlamp.

Couple neighborhood dogs going crazy,

Baying at trespass and missed opportunity.

Frothing mindlessly from years of obedience training.

One of the rats, fatally wounded, fell down

Into the yard of such beast.

Ripped to shreds.

The surviving fiend in victory traipses along further

Until another shows as if from nowhere to steal its claim

There go the dogs again.

Resting Place of the Last Tree Spirit

I had to be even more quiet than normal. Long done are the days of my free reign and roam. Hoards of unsightly life plundered what's mine, insignificant and hairless things. I've remained hidden for too long. Paradise, I once had paradise. 'Tis true nothing lasts forever.

Lonely, indifferent sighs of wind my only company. Once, a small girl came to me. She started conversation. She was nice, the last friend I would ever have. Possibly the only, for that matter. She died long ago; fell sick before she could start a family of her own. I watched her grow over the years, and she taught me many things. But I could see. Sour men plunder spoils of my land. Whilst the fairy folk and mystic beasts I once protected dwindled; their past lost. Tides of progress too much to cross for most of us, methinks.

I had the spiders and beetles to bore me with the yarns they'd spin. Woodland creatures seek on me short respite, content, safe. Dew drops glisten pink in the sun's final seconds of the day. Beautiful, abhorrent, serene, and gut-wrenching. Smoke on the horizon, they were gaining ground. Distant rumbles sent a shiver down my spine.

My head and throat have near constant tickling. Shallow have become both my breath and breadth, as well as the branches on my head. My roots, they have suffered the worst. Once normal for me to trek vast space in a single night, all my might fails to move me far yet. My head and throat have near constant tickling. Dusted breeze bates me, lingering on with hate and ill-temper.

My kingdom, once vast, instead lies in wait. Waiting for my return. It doesn't realize I've never left. Puny man encroaches and stirs me from my slumber. A woman surveys my hidden gardens. She felt like home. My friend. I tried to speak but I couldn't. Could she be the one to save me? My scant, few acres

I called home? Perhaps she was destined to help it grow. To help bring back the fairy folk.

She looked at me, at my soul. I could feel her touch as she smiled. I towered over the forest; she knew I was special. Now I have all sorts of friends. They stay with me from time to time, inside. I cannot speak to them for I'm just a shell. Gutted and hollow her intentions. Carved in my flesh, a place of solitude. Of profit. People stay in here for rest, for better moods.

None shall come to me.

Retirees in Suburbia

Rice paddies, hollow tree stump, and a gentle breeze

slowly climbing flooded meadow floor for better view.

Taking time to ensure even the faintest of things gets ample
thought,

erstwhile vigor shelled away 'round plated joints.

Lest tortoise stone inhibit others nearby they shamble

off. Only after such periods of rest a maimed waterbug

would scoff at. Nary midday and the armored reptiles have
barely budged.

Watching from a buoyant stretch of wood and bark, looking
somehow

down on harvester as it shades the lowly pair. One stares

back at the other, slow-motion blinks and yawn.

About that time again. The harvester stumbled onto the level

below, likely broke its toes, if not more or worse.

Several minutes after they look at the wrecked creature
beneath,

tortoise and the like rest for more slow movements.

<u>Satire</u>

Other day, my daughter asked me about satires-
I told her buck up, and change her thought process.
Why not say 'happy tires' instead?

Other day, my great-grandmother said she was 'sad, tired.'
I had asked how she was.
I told her I wasn't, not one bit. I had only just finished
marathon training, on not much sleep.
But her, that I understood. She had it really bad, what with all
the free meals, sitting down, and shuffleboard. That's just too
much going on.

<u>Snail - Snails</u>

Hard-backed and slow-moving

Pebbles breathing

Shimmering memories forget what they once were

Tender-footed and hungry

Immature and basic

Timid pasts fear not their future

Vanished ego and intent

Quick slickened paths

Spiraling into pain lest it defy

Numbers growing two from one

Life redefined

Unto itself henceforth emanated

Onwards yonder gravel

Fixed from afar

Closer causation reveals bittersweet

Solitude decays swift

Netherlings sounds faint

Tranquil upend to viral penchant

Spanish Inquisition

Tom: I just wanted to help people, at first. Sure, it was fun making something, but- but it just wasn't worth it.

Jerry: Sure. That's where I started, too.

Tom: Then the rumors started, and people misunderstood things, and jokes were taken out of context, and *other* people *were* saying and doing the same things, but *I* wasn't. But it didn't matter.

Jerry: Never does.

Tom: Not one bit.

Jerry: No, sir.

Tom: At the end of the day, aren't we all like a cat chasing a mouse which is natural, and what it was intended for, only to be declawed. They *laughed* at me. Then got angry. *Really* angry. I was only trying to entertain them. Never said I was perfect.

Jerry: You don't have to, it's what they demanded.

Tom: Even still, I tried my best.

Jerry: Like the rest of us.

Tom: I'm not a violent guy, not one bit. I try to do the right thing.

Jerry: We all were.

Tom: I- I just-

Jerry:

Tom: I just never expected this.

Jerry: Nobody does.

The Hunt

Whitetail poofs and traipses in the sticks;

You can lose sight of the agile.

Pay too close attention, however, and some jackass can sneak up

  and have his way. Introduce themselves first, no worries, after

  helping his-or-herself to some peanuts and cheese crackers.

Think you see some antlers, can't tell from the leafless twigs and branch before

Your sights. Distractions do not cease in their bid, but point to the

elephant in the room-

Unbeknownst to even the savviest surveyors of forest and stream,

The honeybees vanishing, not that anyone could tell from sweat and mason,

Plentiful enough to dupe captain and foot soldier, alike.

Quail and chaparral cock flee as the deer grunts and bellows,

Stood on its hindquarters and exposed its ribs, bemused and knackered.

The Juror

Ogred nostrils flare twain

Like Quasimodo lunkered down from atop

Belltower cage, plotting

Escape from enmassed throngs

Thumb-twiddling bestilled ansgt in air

Crunching to pass the time

Ravenous and ill-raised

Fools spraying crumbs about

A few pieces stuck in ogrish brow

Sitting on his stump, looks like a small pebble

'Neath ursine king

Royal service anew his craft

Muttering converse and trivialities

Considering which bunkmate would taste best ground

And baked into toast

Mannered beast save deceit

Peering to his right

Ear to ear, he smiles at me

His decision made

The Necklace

Don furrowed brow upon first glance

Entranced by the cursed jewel, lusting

These affairs shone through the decay and modern quaintness

Servers averted their stares elsewhere

Too much for the night temptress

No cages, no prisons; exposition

Glamour and gawd dare not forbid her request

By night's own, lest to pause

Lone she entered, leaving courted

Dangling, soaking the night sky like a sponge

Unadulterated beauty recognizes itself, no need for mirror

To feel alive, such like a harlot, or queen

The silver slivers perfectly grasp her throat

Black eyes look from her reflection

Willow trees reach out their fingertips, futilely

The necklace emboldens its grip

Blood starts trickling down her neck

Malintent begets the grain as razorwire

Spinning, and spinning, and spinning

Sin comes only but for the cursed

Blood-curling screams turn to gurgle

Loses feeling in her legs, collapses

Relapses often prove mistake

View jolts back to cloud, fading

For she entered lone, in the end crowds drown out her soul

Face locked in tight envy of those circled

Witness winter's end, beauty's rebirth

Mouth full of dirt, tempting those to goddess' fate

<u>things i've seen the last two days</u>

Green scarab beetles, two different kinds

Once solid white flower buds reveal now magenta kissed

blooms

Evening time, teal explosion in the skies like an atomic bomb

St. Elmo's fire aghast

Tidal-waved wind hits like a freight train, house pelleted by

ripe walnuts in droves

Then came the rain

And more rain

Fine, dancing mist evading large droplets like dancing fae

Clear skies after the storm

Mother Moon greets the sun in morn

Ducking from a young red-tailed hawk as it drops just inches

away

Next, and not to be outdone, two green parrots squawked and

frolicked

In the skies, overhead

Very next stop, winged ants flap and flutter off, scraping

themselves away from termite foe

Most make it past, but then must contend with the dragons

Their king, gold and green, clutching the small ants with its

jaws

Dragonflies rule the day, a half dozen or so more across the

way

Fire that night, flickers contrast the shadowed figures against

the fence

My wife beside me, hand in hand in wine

It's fine

Triumph

Tiring

Turning

Trumped

Dumped

Duped

Bloated bump

Frumpy

Crunk

Funk

Fuck

Grump

Trumpets blast

Lumped

Tons

Irons

Tires

Tree stumps

Triumph

Enough

Enough

Enough

Enough

<u>Vera</u>

From afar you seem so genuine

I sense a darkness preying effortless

A foot in front of foot of other

We are just like one another

Sun brightens nightfall into day

I pray again for whom to meet

Beside me past the hedgerow

Growing old as justly oaks

Spoken as if it were ever to happen

Circumstantial needs pretend yet I cannot rely on them

Soft lips caress the wind whisper blown reed

Darkened skies but i can see the fireflies

Seizing and with elegance dwindle dimly

Fading into night

I see you from afar

You shine at times

Reflect the moon's passion

I stay silent

Observing yet

Vulture Blue

Blistered teeth gnash and grind on brittle decay
    Hollow bones fester negativity and taut figure, hiding in
crumbling walls
        Hunger pangs knot and twist as enameled force
    Scavenged morsels like fury
            Those other jagged knuckles
dragging down the rest
    Social circles fall victim to disparate reflected gaze
Rotten flesh sustains no more than filth
        Waiting in rafter to swoop the gains of others

<u>What happened to the other one?</u>

Back when times were simple,

Adolescent friendships and self-discovery

Grew into something lasting

At least I thought so.

Never did I think I would be able to give it another chance

So many years after. But there it was

New and different. Couldn't pick my finger on it at first

Often, I listen to how he enunciates, sounds forced

Like he's afraid of losing any credibility to the matter.

I feel like someone is missing, maybe that's what's different

Keep getting distracted by antics and false scenes

Ears deceive, both digital and physical

Granting allusion to the puppet strings

Retrograde actions deceived me, because I believe

Others don't.

Forget what you think you know

Frail egos collide all the time, and only one person can win in a grudge match.

<u>What If Israel?</u>

What if they lied?

What if they murdered?

What if they were honest about it?

What if the villains were heroes?

What if people are wrong?

What if they hide?

What if they flaunt?

What if magick?

What if it's not real?

What if Israel?

<u>You don't think someone else took over and is now doing the same thing?</u>

Enter now from golden goose' charm

Perchance swayed by glistening harbors of

Scintillations

Tactful yet unnerved against elitist grip

No one stranger, spider web threaded

Of dreaded consequence and thought

Surely those whispers frown now

Ultimately escaping jaded views

In the valleys of lust and power

Concerns so far above laymen knowledge

Dead-souled and gaping, plucking chicken feathers

"The individual has always had to struggle to
keep from being overwhelmed by the tribe. If you
try it, you will be lonely often, and sometimes
frightened. But no price is too high to pay for the
privilege of owning yourself."

- Rudyard Kipling

www.ingramcontent.com/pod-product-compliance
Lightning Source LLC
Chambersburg PA
CBHW071618150726
48000CB00004B/1772